EVERYDAY
SPECIALS

Contents

ACKNOWLEDGMENTS

Executive Editor - Nick Rowe

Cookery Editor - Sarah Lumley

Food Preparation - Sarah Lumley, Elaine Bastable and Jenny Shapter

Wine advisor - David Wrigley MW

Photography - Graham Langridge

Design and Illustrations - Amba Design

Production - John Vanner

Printing - Jarrold Printing

Published by
Milk Marque Limited
Product Development Centre,
Reaseheath,
Nantwich, Cheshire.
CW5 6TA

BAKED HADDOCK IN CRÈME FRAÎCHE
PAGE 50

COOKERY EDITOR

"Dear Reader,
Welcome to Everyday Specials,
an all new edition from the Dairy Book of Home Cookery range.

There were two reasons for producing this new book.
The first has been the many hundreds of letters we receive each year,
requesting copies of previous editions and asking when
new books will be published.

The second is from my own experience. In preparing recipes for the
Dairy Diary, I found that what cooks really want are recipes which are
straight forward and easy to prepare, but just that little bit different.
With preparation and cooking times of under 45 minutes,
each of the sixty recipes is quick enough for everyday
and I hope you will agree, that they all look and taste extra special.

All the recipes use ingredients which can be bought at your
local supermarket or independent food store and don't forget
to ask your milkman what he can deliver.
As seasoning is usually down to personal preference I haven't included
it in every recipe, only where I feel it is essential.
With the exception of those that dry so well (Rosemary, Thyme...),
I recommend the use of fresh herbs. If you find them difficult
to obtain - nag your local shop manager!

Each recipe is clearly laid out for you to follow, with the ingredients boldly
listed and the method set out in points for easy reference.
You could even take the book with you when shopping for ingredients.

A cook's tip accompanies each recipe which may suggest
alternatives or provide extra information to make the recipe easier.
As preparation and cooking times will influence your choice of dish
these are clearly identified and range from 10 to 45 minutes.
Every recipe has been tested at least three times,
so you can be confident they work!
The recipe information is based on an average serving
and is approximate, as different brands and styles of product
have varied compositions.
Calories have been calculated to the nearest five.

Food and drink go hand in hand, so every recipe includes
a drink recommendation which vary from soft drinks to wine.
I find that wine is still treated as a very serious affair
shrouded in mystery and misunderstanding.
My wine recommendations are purely personal but
they do carry the approval of David Wrigley a Master of Wine
from the Wine and Spirit Education Trust.
There isn't room to go into too much detail but I feel the notes
will give sufficient guidance and inspiration.

A good dish does not necessarily need hours of preparation,
copious sauces and fancy garnishes.
What it does require however, are quality ingredients,
planning, good company and a sense of humour.

Finally enjoy this book - enjoy your food and
bon appetit!"

Sarah Lumley .

Here is a list of store cupboard ingredients
which will always be useful for making the recipes in this book.
I haven't included the obvious and obscure, but those items
handy for preparing quick easy meals at short notice.

PACKETS

Long grain rice	Risotto rice	Pasta shapes
Pizza base mix	Dried Chinese noodles	Coconut cream
Slivered almonds	Pine kernels	Dried apricots

BOTTLES AND JARS

Extra virgin olive oil	Sesame oil	Black olives
White wine vinegar	Balsamic vinegar	Vegetable stock
Sundried tomato paste	Ginger paste	Mint sauce
Worcester sauce	Hoisin sauce	Soy sauce
Pasta sauce	Chilli sauce	

CANS AND TINS

White and red wine	Chopped tomatoes	Condensed soups
Chilli beans	Sweetcorn	Artichoke hearts
Anchovies	Peaches	Apricots

HERBS AND SPICES

Cumin - ground and seeds	Curry powder	Paprika
Green cardamom pods	Ground coriander	Garlic
Mixed herbs	Caraway seeds	Cinnamon

FREEZER COMPARTMENT

Filo pastry	Puff pastry	Chopped spinach

FRIDGE

Cheddar cheese	Milk	Butter
Parmesan cheese	Natural yogurt	Bacon rashers
Cream cheese		Unwaxed lemons

WEIGHTS AND MEASURES

DRY WEIGHT CONVERSIONS

RECOMMENDED GRAMS (g)	IMPERIAL OUNCES (OZ)
15	1/2
25	1
50	2
75	3
110	4 (1/4 lb)
150	5
175	6
200	7
225	8 (1/2 lb)
250	9
275	10
300	11
350	12 (3/4 lb)
375	13
400	14
425	15
450	16 (1lb)

LIQUID CONVERSIONS

METRIC	IMPERIAL
15ml	1/2 fl oz
30ml	1 fl oz
60ml	2 fl oz
90ml	3 fl oz
125ml	4 fl oz
150ml	5 fl oz (1/4 pint)
175ml	6 fl oz
250ml	8 fl oz
300ml	10 fl oz (1/2 pint)
375ml	12 fl oz
500ml	16 fl oz
600ml	20 fl oz (1 pint)
900ml	1 1/2 pints
1 litre	1 3/4 pints
1 1/4 litre	2 pints
1 1/2 litres	2 1/3 pints
2 litres	3 1/4 pints

These quantities are not exact but calculated to give proportionately correct measurements.

OVEN TEMPERATURE CONVERSIONS

CENTIGRADE°	110	120	140	150	160	180	190	200	220	230	240
FAHRENHEIT°	225	250	275	300	325	350	375	400	425	450	475
GAS NUMBER	1/4	1/2	1	2	3	4	5	6	7	8	9

This guide gives recommended equivalent settings, not exact conversions. Always refer to your cooker handbook.

PASTA NAPOLI

*An Italian classic combination of shallots, garlic and tomatoes which we have
revived with a splash of balsamic vinegar, pungent fresh basil and fresh Pecorino cheese.*

Olive oil	*2 tablespoons*
Shallots	*4, chopped*
Garlic cloves	*3, crushed*
Chopped tomatoes	*1 large tin (400g)*
Tomato purée with basil	*1 tablespoon*
Spaghetti	*375g*
Balsamic vinegar	*2 tablespoons*
Fresh basil	*a large handful*
Pecorino cheese	*40g, freshly grated*

METHOD

1. Heat the oil in a heavy pan and gently sauté
   the shallots until transparent.

2. Add the garlic and stir. Add the tomatoes and tomato purée.
   Cover and simmer whilst you cook the spaghetti.
   Drain and keep warm.

3. Turn up the heat for the tomato sauce and add the vinegar.
   Stir and cook for 1 minute. Add the fresh basil
   which should be roughly torn but kept in large pieces.

4. Serve with the spaghetti, either mixed together or separately.
   Serve the cheese separately with the dish.

TO DRINK	RECIPE INFORMATION	COOK'S TIP
We'd recommend a gentle Italian white wine. Try a chilled Verdicchio, Vernaccia or dry Orvieto.	RECIPE SERVES 4 Preparation - **10 minutes** Cooking - **15 minutes**	Always follow the packet instructions when cooking dried pasta.

AVERAGE VALUES PER PORTION
Calories - 255 kcals
Protein - 6g
Carbohydrate - 5g
Fat - 10g

Overcooked pasta
becomes sticky and
undercooked can be
difficult to digest.

Pasta Napoli

Sweet Potato Stew

Many people are at a loss as to how to serve sweet potatoes.
In our opinion this sweet and spicy dish is an excellent example.

Sweet potatoes	*2, peeled and diced*
Parsnips	*2, peeled and diced*
Oil	*1 tablespoon*
Large onions	*2, sliced*
Cumin seeds	*1 tablespoon*
Ground coriander	*1 tablespoon*
Ginger paste	*1 tablespoon*
Garlic cloves	*3, crushed*
Chilli sauce	*1 teaspoon*
Chopped tomatoes	*1 large tin (400g)*
Fresh parsley	*2 tablespoons, roughly chopped*

METHOD

1. Par boil the sweet potatoes and parsnips for 5 minutes and drain.

2. Heat the oil in a casserole and sauté the onions with the spices for 2-3 minutes.

3. Add the ginger, garlic and chilli sauce and stir.

4. Add the vegetables and chopped tomatoes. Cover and cook for 20 minutes.

5. Take off the heat, stir and then serve decorated with chopped parsley.

TO DRINK

The Italian white wine Pinot Grigio, complements the ginger in this dish, as does the light red, Côtes du Rhône.

RECIPE INFORMATION

RECIPE SERVES 4

Preparation - **15 minutes**
Cooking - **20 minutes**

AVERAGE VALUES PER PORTION
Calories - 295 kcals
Protein - 6g
Carbohydrate - 60g
Fat - 5g

COOK'S TIP

To stop sweet potatoes and parsnips going brown when peeled, leave them in cold water with a teaspoon of lemon juice.

SWEET POTATO STEW

CHEDDAR ENCHILADAS

A hot and spicy Mexican speciality - using the best English cheese!

FILLING

Onion	*1 large, finely chopped*
Sunflower oil	*1 tablespoon*
Garlic cloves	*3, crushed*
Chilli powder	*½ teaspoon*
Ground cumin	*2 teaspoons*
Chopped tomatoes with herbs	*1 large tin (400g)*
Tomato purée	*1 tablespoon*
Chilli beans	*1 small tin (215g), drained*

TOPPING

Flour tortillas	*8*
Cheddar cheese	*200g, grated*
Fresh coriander	*3 tablespoons, chopped 1 tablespoon for garnish*
Avocado	*1, diced and coated in*
Lemon juice	*1 tablespoon*
Soured cream	*4 tablespoons*

METHOD

1. Fry the onion in the oil for 3 minutes until transparent. Add the garlic and spices, cook for 1 minute then add the tomatoes and tomato purée.

2. Simmer uncovered for at least 10 minutes to allow the juice to reduce then add the chilli beans and take off the heat. Preheat the oven to 180°C.

3. Fill each tortilla with a heaped tablespoon of the sauce and top with 2 tablespoons of cheese and some coriander. Roll the tortillas like a pancake and pack together in a greased baking dish. Bake for 20 minutes. Heat the remaining chilli sauce and spoon into a warmed serving bowl.

4. Garnish with the avocado, soured cream and remaining coriander. Serve the remaining Cheddar in a separate dish with the bowl of sauce.

TO DRINK

Try a soft and flavoursome red wine from Southern Italy, Sardinia or Sicily.

RECIPE INFORMATION

RECIPE SERVES 4

Preparation - **20 minutes**
Cooking - **20 minutes**

AVERAGE VALUES PER PORTION
Calories - 740 kcals
Protein - 28g
Carbohydrate - 86g
Fat - 33g

COOK'S TIP

For a more 'fiery' dish. use a fresh red chilli. Using the seeds as well makes it much hotter.

CHEDDAR ENCHILADAS

CHEESE FONDUE WITH A VEGETABLE MEDLEY

A collection of roasted and fresh vegetables dipped in this rich cheese sauce makes a good sociable meal.

TO DIP	FONDUE
Courgette *1 cubed*	**Garlic cloves** *2, crushed*
Onion *1 large, roughly chopped*	**Olive oil** *1 tablespoon*
Button mushrooms *25g, wiped*	**White wine** *250ml*
Olive oil *2 tablespoons*	**Cornflour** *1 tablespoon*
Foccacia bread *1 loaf, cubed*	**English Cheddar** *200g, grated*
Red pepper *1, cubed*	**Red Leicester cheese** *250g, grated*
Celery sticks *2, sliced into wedges*	**Fresh parsley** *3 tablespoons, chopped*
Apples *2, cubed and coated in* **Lemon juice** *2 tablespoons*	**Fresh chives** · *10 blades, snipped*

METHOD

1. Preheat the oven to 200°C. Roast the courgette, onion and mushrooms in 2 tablespoons of olive oil for 5 minutes. Bake the bread for 5 minutes, then turn off the heat. Leave the vegetables and bread in the oven to keep hot.

2. Meanwhile mix the garlic and olive oil together and smear around the inside of the fondue. Light the fondue according to the instructions.

3. Mix the white wine and cornflour in a cup and add to the fondue, heating gently and stirring occasionally. When the wine starts to steam add the cheese and stir constantly so that it starts to melt and thicken. Heat until thickened, add the herbs and turn down the heat to minimum.

4. Serve with the roasted and raw vegetables, warmed bread and apples.

TO DRINK	RECIPE INFORMATION	COOK'S TIPS
Aromatic dry white wines are excellent with this fondue. Try a Sauvignon Blanc or Riesling from the New World.	RECIPE SERVES 4 Preparation - **15 minutes** Cooking - **20 minutes** AVERAGE VALUES PER PORTION Calories - 855 kcals Protein - 37g Carbohydrate - 50g Fat - 54g	Cheese fondue originated from Switzerland, but this recipe makes the most of English territorials. Flat skewers ensure the vegetables and bread don't swivel around and fall off.

CHEESE FONDUE WITH A VEGETABLE MEDLEY

CHEATS LASAGNE

Quick and simple - this lasagne uses a rich ricotta filling with fresh vegetables.

Ricotta cheese	*2 tubs (250g)*
Milk	*150ml*
Parmesan cheese	*75g, grated (reserve 2 tbsp for the top)*
Black pepper	*to season*
Nutmeg	*1 teaspoon*
Tomato pasta sauce	*500g*
Lasagne sheets	*8 (no pre-cooking required)*
Courgettes	*3, sliced*
Mushrooms	*125g, sliced*
Leeks	*2, sliced into rings*
Fresh parsley	*3 tablespoons, chopped*
Fresh oregano	*1 tablespoon, chopped*
Mozzarella cheese	*150g, sliced thinly*

METHOD

1. Preheat oven to 200°C. Mix the ricotta with the milk, Parmesan, pepper and nutmeg.

2. Spoon 5 tablespoons of tomato pasta sauce into the lasagne dish and place half the lasagne sheets over the sauce.

3. Spoon half the ricotta mixture over the sheets and then top with the vegetables. Add the remaining pasta sauce, herbs and mozzarella. Repeat the layer of pasta sheets. Top with the remaining ricotta mix and Parmesan.

4. Cover with foil and bake for 30 minutes. Remove the foil, turn the heat down to 190°C and bake for a further 5 minutes and serve.

TO DRINK

The herbs and tomato sauce in this dish are complemented by a wine such as Vin de Pays des Côtes de Gascogne, or alternatively choose a Chianti.

RECIPE INFORMATION

RECIPE SERVES 4
Preparation - **10 minutes**
Cooking - **35 minutes**

AVERAGE VALUES PER PORTION
Calories - 645 kcals
Protein - 38g
Carbohydrate - 50g
Fat - 34g

COOK'S TIP

It is important to start the layering of your lasagne with the sauce. This ensures that all the lasagne used is covered, on top and bottom with moisture.

CHEATS LASAGNE

RED LENTILS WITH ONIONS

*One of the best vegetarian curries - bursting with flavour,
wholesome and great as a main course or a side dish.*

Butter	*25g*
Onions	*2, chopped*
Garlic cloves	*2, crushed*
Turmeric	*1 teaspoon*
Curry powder	*2 teaspoons*
Red lentils	*225g, rinsed well*
Vegetable stock	*450ml*
Naan bread	*to accompany*
Fresh coriander	*4 tablespoons, roughly chopped*

METHOD

1. Melt the butter in a casserole and fry the onions
until brown and crispy on the edges.
Add the garlic and spices and stir.

2. Add the lentils and stock and bring to the boil.
Simmer for 30 minutes, stirring occasionally.

3. Warm the naan bread according to the packet instructions.

4. Stir the coriander into the lentils and serve at once
in warmed bowls with the naan bread.

TO DRINK

The popular drink with curry is chilled lager.

For wine, choose a soft inexpensive Australian or Bulgarian red.

RECIPE INFORMATION

RECIPE SERVES 4

Preparation - **5 minutes**
Cooking - **30 minutes**

AVERAGE VALUES PER PORTION
Calories - 255 kcals
Protein - 15g
Carbohydrate - 38g
Fat - 6g

COOK'S TIPS

Lentils, unlike dried beans and pulses, do not need to be soaked before cooking.

However, rinse them thoroughly in a colander and discard any shrivelled lentils or bits of grit.

RED LENTILS WITH ONIONS

SPINACH FILO PIE

A wholesome medley of vegetables with Feta cheese nestled between layers of crisp, golden filo pastry.

Large onion	*1, finely chopped*
Olive oil	*3 tablespoons*
Dried mixed herbs	*1 heaped teaspoon*
Frozen chopped spinach	*650g, defrosted*
Feta cheese	*150g, crumbled*
Curd cheese	*110g*
Black pepper	*to season*
Filo pastry	*200g*
Butter	*25g, melted*
Tomatoes	*2, cut into thin wedges*
Black olives	*12, pitted*

METHOD

1. Fry the onion in 2 tablespoons of oil for 3 minutes. Add the mixed herbs and spinach and cook gently for a further 3 minutes.

2. Mix the two cheeses and carefully fold them into the spinach mixture with some black pepper. Preheat the oven to 180°C.

3. Brush a lasagne style dish 25 x 20 cm *(10 x 8 inch)*, with the remaining oil. Brush 3 sheets of filo with butter and place in the dish ensuring they cover the base and overlap the edge a little.

4. Spread the spinach mixture over the filo base and add the tomatoes and olives.

5. Brush the remaining sheets generously with butter and scrunch them up. Cover the vegetables with the filo and bake in the oven for 10-15 minutes.

TO DRINK

Two Italian white wines provide the best accompaniment to spinach - a difficult vegetable to partner - Frascati and Soave.

RECIPE INFORMATION

RECIPE SERVES 4

Preparation - **10 minutes**
Cooking - **15 minutes**

AVERAGE VALUES PER PORTION
Calories - 540 kcals
Protein - 21g
Carbohydrate - 41g
Fat - 33g

COOK'S TIP

When preparing your dish, keep the leaves of filo pastry you're not working with covered so they don't crack and dry out.

SPINACH FILO PIE

Courgette and Leek Bake

A hearty vegetarian winter warmer - making the most of fresh vegetables.

Olive oil	*1 tablespoon*
Garlic cloves	*2, crushed*
Vegetable stock	*125ml*
Baking potato	*1, peeled and cubed*
Leeks	*3, washed, trimmed and sliced*
Courgettes	*3, washed, trimmed and sliced*
Dried mixed herbs	*1 teaspoon*
Double Gloucester cheese	*225g, grated*
Cream cheese	*200g*
Fresh milk	*2 tablespoons*
Paprika	*1 teaspoon*

METHOD

1. Heat the oil and gently sauté the garlic. Add the stock and potato, cover and cook for 5 minutes. Add the leeks and courgettes, cover and cook for 3 minutes. Preheat the oven to 220°C.

2. Uncover the pan and simmer for 4 minutes, until the liquid has almost been absorbed. Spoon the vegetable mix into a greased ovenproof serving dish.

3. Place half the Double Gloucester with the cream cheese, milk and paprika into a bowl and mix well.

4. Spoon the cheese mixture over the vegetables and sprinkle the remaining Double Gloucester over the dish. Bake for 15 minutes until golden.

TO DRINK

A simple chilled beer goes well with this hearty dish, or you could try a soft Spanish red from La Mancha or Valdepeñas.

RECIPE INFORMATION

RECIPE SERVES 4

Preparation - **15 minutes**
Cooking - **15 minutes**

AVERAGE VALUES PER PORTION
Calories - 620 kcals
Protein - 22g
Carbohydrate - 30g
Fat - 47g

COOK'S TIP

When sautéing garlic, be careful not to let it brown. When this occurs the garlic becomes bitter in taste.

COURGETTE AND LEEK BAKE

CARROT AND CORIANDER SALAD

A colourful salad which can be served at any time of year.

DRESSING

Fresh orange juice	*4 tablespoons*
Sunflower oil	*4 tablespoons*
White wine vinegar	*2 tablespoons*
Lime cordial	*1 teaspoon*
Sesame oil	*1 teaspoon*
Worcester sauce	*½ teaspoon*

SALAD

Spinach	*1 bag (approx. 250g)*
Carrots	*200g, peeled*
Oranges	*3, peeled and sliced into segments*
Fresh coriander	*1 handful, leaves only*
Avocado	*1 large, ripe*

METHOD

1. Whisk the dressing ingredients together in a jug.

2. Remove the stems from the spinach leaves and rinse, then place in a large salad bowl.

3. Grate the carrots in a food processor or by hand. Add to the spinach with the orange segments and coriander.

4. Peel and dice the avocado and carefully fold into the salad mixture. Pour 4-5 tablespoons of dressing over the salad and serve.

TO DRINK

A chilled French white wine from the Loire region, such as Sancerre will go down a treat with this salad.

RECIPE INFORMATION

RECIPE SERVES 4

Preparation - **10 minutes**
Cooking - **none**

AVERAGE VALUES PER PORTION
Calories - 335 kcals
Protein - 7g
Carbohydrate - 20g
Fat - 26g

COOK'S TIP

To find out if an avocado is ripe, press gently at the top of the fruit. If it is slightly soft it is ripe. There is no need to press the whole fruit since it will bruise and go brown.

CARROT AND CORIANDER SALAD

GARLIC MUSHROOM PIZZA

*A mixture of mushrooms with the whole roasted garlic cloves and lightly roasted herbs
makes a simple, wholesome vegetarian feast.*

MAKES 2 x 26 CM (10 INCH) PIZZAS

Pizza base mix	*2 packets*
Mild onions	*2, cut into 8 pieces*
Garlic cloves	*10, whole and unpeeled*
Olive oil	*3 tablespoons, plus 2 extra tablespoons*
Mushrooms	*250g, sliced*
Black pepper	*to season*
Fresh thyme	*a handful of sprigs*

METHOD

1. Make up the pizza base dough as instructed on the packet.
Turn the dough onto a floured surface and knead until smooth.

2. Preheat the oven to 200°C. Place the onion pieces and garlic cloves
into a roasting tin and drizzle with 3 tablespoons of olive oil.
Roast for 5 minutes until starting to brown.

3. Roll out the pizza dough to make two bases about 26 cm in diameter.
Place each base on a non-stick pizza pan or baking tray.

4. Arrange the roasted onions, garlic cloves and mushrooms on the bases.

5. Drizzle generously with the remaining olive oil, season with black pepper
and bake for 12 minutes. Scatter the thyme over the pizzas and
bake for a further 3-4 minutes until the edges are golden.

TO DRINK

New Zealand or
Californian
Pinot Noir wines will
complement the roasted
onions and garlic.
Alternatively go for a
light, fruity Beaujolais.

RECIPE INFORMATION

RECIPE SERVES 4
Preparation - **20 minutes**
Cooking - **15 minutes**

AVERAGE VALUES PER PORTION
Calories - 430 kcals
Protein - 10g
Carbohydrate - 52g
Fat - 20g

COOK'S TIP

Add a teaspoon of olive oil
and a teaspoon of dried
mixed herbs to the pizza
base whilst you
are kneading
it, to add
extra flavour.

GARLIC MUSHROOM PIZZA

SMOKED MACARONI CHEESE

Find a cheese shop and buy the best Farmhouse Smoked Cheddar - this dish deserves it!

Cauliflower	*400g, cut into small florets*
Macaroni	*350g*
Sunflower oil	*2 tablespoons*
Large onion	*1, thinly sliced*
Milk	*90ml, plus 500ml*
Flour	*3 tablespoons*
Nutmeg	*pinch*
Smoked Cheddar	*225g, grated*
Fresh parsley	*3 tablespoons, chopped*

METHOD

1. Blanch the cauliflower in boiling water, remove with a slotted spoon and place in a greased ovenproof dish, reserving the water to cook the macaroni.

2. Cook the macaroni as instructed on the pack. Drain and add to the cauliflower.

3. Preheat the oven to 190°C. Meanwhile, heat the oil and sauté the onion until brown. Lower the heat and add 90ml milk, the flour and nutmeg. Mix vigorously to form a soft paste.

4. Gradually add the extra milk to make a white sauce. As the sauce starts to thicken, stir with a whisk to smooth any lumps and carefully add the cheese in batches, reserving a heaped tablespoon for later.

5. Once the sauce is thick and the cheese has melted, pour over the macaroni and cauliflower and bake in the oven for 15 minutes. Sprinkle with the remaining cheese and parsley and serve.

TO DRINK

An oaked Californian or Australian Chardonnay go best with a sauce made with smoked Cheddar. For a red wine, try Rioja or Chianti.

RECIPE INFORMATION

RECIPE SERVES 4

Preparation - **15 minutes**
Cooking - **15 minutes**

AVERAGE VALUES PER PORTION
Calories - 535 kcals
Protein - 26g
Carbohydrate - 37g
Fat - 32g

COOK'S TIP

Use finely grated cheese to make this sauce. This ensures that only a low heat is necessary to melt the cheese which will prevent it becoming grainy through over cooking.

SMOKED MACARONI CHEESE

Tomato, Basil and Artichoke Tart

A light pastry base topped with the freshest tomatoes and basil with sweet artichoke hearts.

Puff pastry   *400g packet, ready made*

Sundried tomato paste   *2 tablespoons*

Fresh tomatoes   *400g, sliced*

Tinned artichoke hearts   *4, drained, rinsed and quartered*

Fresh basil   *1 handful, leaving some for a garnish*

Fresh Parmesan   *25g, pared*

Black pepper   *to season*

Balsamic vinegar   *1 teaspoon*

METHOD

1. Preheat the oven to 220°C.

2. Roll out the pastry and cut out a circle about 30 cm *(12 inch)* diameter.
Place onto a greased baking sheet.

3. Leaving a 2.5 cm *(1 inch)* border around the edge,
smear the tomato paste over the pastry.

4. Place the tomatoes and artichokes over the pastry, covering the tomato paste.
Tear the basil leaves and scatter over the tomatoes with the Parmesan
and finally season with plenty of freshly milled black pepper.

5. Bake in the oven for 15-18 minutes until golden.
Splash the balsamic vinegar sparingly over the tart and serve hot,
decorated with the extra basil.

TO DRINK

Fruit cordials diluted with carbonated spring water go well - or a robust red wine such as a Bairrada from Portugal.

RECIPE INFORMATION

RECIPE SERVES 4

Preparation - **10 minutes**
Cooking - **18 minutes**

AVERAGE VALUES PER PORTION
Calories - 635 kcals
Protein - 9g
Carbohydrate - 54g
Fat - 44g

COOK'S TIPS

Serve at once so the pastry does not go soggy.

Buy the best quality balsamic vinegar that you can afford - you will need less of it.

TOMATO, BASIL AND ARTICHOKE TART

PUMPKIN CURRY

Now you know what to do with this obscure vegetable!

Pumpkin	*650g*
Sunflower oil	*2 tablespoons*
Red chilli	*1, deseeded and finely chopped*
Garlic cloves	*2, thinly sliced*
Ground cumin	*2 teaspoons*
Garam Masala	*1 tablespoon*
Onion	*1, chopped*
Chopped tomatoes	*1 large tin (400g)*
Vegetable stock	*100ml*
Sweetcorn	*1 small tin (200g), drained*
Peas	*110g, defrosted*
Fresh coriander	*3 tablespoons, chopped*

METHOD

1. Peel the pumpkin and remove the pith and seeds. Rinse and dice into bite size cubes.

2. Bring the pumpkin to the boil and simmer for 5 minutes and then drain.

3. In a separate pan, heat the oil and stir fry the chilli, garlic and spices for 30 seconds. Add the onion and fry for 2 minutes.

4. Stir well and add the pumpkin and tomatoes, stir and add the stock. Bring to the boil and simmer, partially covered for 20 minutes.

5. Add the sweetcorn and peas and cook for 10 minutes uncovered. Scatter the coriander over the dish and serve at once.

TO DRINK

A touch of sweetness in the wine will match the pumpkin and temper the spice, so choose a medium white from Germany.

RECIPE INFORMATION

RECIPE SERVES 4

Preparation - **15 minutes**
Cooking - **30 minutes**

AVERAGE VALUES PER PORTION
Calories - 180 kcals
Protein - 6g
Carbohydrate - 23g
Fat - 8g

COOK'S TIP

Pumpkin is a winter squash with a thick skin and sweet flesh. Other winter squashes could be used i.e. butternut or acorn.

PUMPKIN CURRY

Pizza Niçoise

A departure from the usual varieties of pizza, this seafood feast is a favourite.

Ready made 'boboli' style pizza bases *2 (approx. 23 cm / 9 inch)*

Sundried tomato paste *4 tablespoons*

Tomatoes *3, sliced*

Tinned tuna *200g, drained*

Squid *3, cleaned, sliced into thin rings*

Mozzarella *175g, thinly sliced*

Red onion *1, sliced into rings*

Black olives *12, pitted*

Garlic cloves *2, crushed*

Anchovies *4, finely sliced*

Fresh basil *4 tablespoons, roughly torn*

Dried oregano *1 teaspoon*

Black pepper *to season*

Extra virgin olive oil *2 tablespoons*

METHOD

1. Preheat the oven to 190°C. Meanwhile smear the tomato paste over the pizza bases and top with the tomatoes.

2. Place chunks of tuna on the tomatoes and surround with the squid rings.

3. Top the pizza with the slices of mozzarella, red onion, olives, garlic, anchovies and finally the basil. Season with the dried oregano, black pepper and drizzle the oil over the pizzas.

4. Place in the oven and cook for 7-9 minutes.

TO DRINK

The rich tomato, herb and garlic flavours really suggest a red wine, despite the fish. Try a Barbera from Piedmont.

RECIPE INFORMATION

RECIPE SERVES 4
Preparation - **10 minutes**
Cooking - **9 minutes**

AVERAGE VALUES PER PORTION
Calories - 780 kcals
Protein - 35g
Carbohydrate - 71g
Fat - 39g

COOK'S TIP

Make sure you buy smaller squid for this dish which won't go tough when they are cooked.

PIZZA NIÇOISE

FENNEL AND PRAWN STIR FRY

The aniseed flavour of the fennel with a generous splash of Pernod produce a stunningly flavoured dish.

Olive oil	*3 tablespoons*
Cooked king prawns	*300g, peeled*
Sundried tomato paste	*2 tablespoons*
Fennel bulbs	*3, trimmed and sliced*
Pernod or Ricard	*6 tablespoons*
Black pepper	*to season*
Fennel fronds	*to decorate*

METHOD

1. Heat the olive oil in a wok on a high heat.

2. Rinse the prawns under cold water.

3. Mix the prawns with the tomato paste and add to the wok. Stir constantly for 2 minutes then turn down the heat.

4. Add the fennel bulbs and Pernod and continue to stir fry for 4 minutes.

5. Season with the pepper, decorate with the fennel fronds and serve hot with lots of fresh crusty bread.

TO DRINK

Delicate wines will wilt under the strength of flavours and aroma from this rich dish. An aromatic dry Riesling from Alsace or Australia would work well.

RECIPE INFORMATION

RECIPE SERVES 4

Preparation - **10 minutes**
Cooking - **6 minutes**

AVERAGE VALUES PER PORTION
Calories - 275 kcals
Protein - 15g
Carbohydrate - 16g
Fat - 13g

COOK'S TIP

If king prawns are beyond your budget, tiger prawns or ordinary Atlantic prawns can be used instead.

FENNEL AND PRAWN STIR FRY

SMOKED MUSSEL PASTA

A most unusual but flavoursome dish, quick and simple to serve.

Smoked mussels	*2 tins (105g), drained*
Fresh coriander	*5 tablespoons, chopped*
Garlic cloves	*3, sliced*
Linguine	*300g*
Double cream	*75ml*
Black pepper	*to season*
Lime	*1, sliced to decorate*

METHOD

1. Mix the smoked mussels with the coriander and garlic. Cover and set aside.

2. Cook the linguine according to the pack instructions. Drain and place into a large warmed serving bowl.

3. Add the double cream and black pepper and stir. Top with the mussel mixture, fold in gently and serve immediately.

TO DRINK

A Gewurztraminer d'Alsace is an excellent accompaniment to both the mussels and cream and would also stand up to the garlic.

RECIPE INFORMATION

RECIPE SERVES 4

Preparation - **5 minutes**
Cooking - **10 minutes**

AVERAGE VALUES PER PORTION
Calories - 415 kcals
Protein - 19g
Carbohydrate - 4g
Fat - 66g

COOK'S TIP

For those who are not garlic lovers, cut the amount down. The garlic flavour in this dish is very prominent, simply because it is raw.

SMOKED MUSSEL PASTA

FISH KEBABS

A wonderful way of enjoying seafood and very easy to prepare and serve.

Tiger prawns	*24, uncooked*
Scallops	*8*
Monkfish tail	*250g*
Fennel	*1 bulb*
Cherry tomatoes	*16*
Mild onion	*1, quartered*
Oil	*1 tablespoon*
Salt	*to season*
Dried herbes de Provence	*2 teaspoons*

METHOD

1. Soak 8 wooden kebab skewers in water for at least 15 minutes.

2. Rinse the prawns, scallops and monkfish under cold water. Cut the monkfish into large chunks.

3. Chop the fennel into chunky bite size pieces.

4. Preheat the grill to a medium-hot heat and line a grill pan with foil.

5. Thread the fish and vegetables onto the skewers. Brush with the oil, season and then sprinkle the dried herbs generously over the kebabs.

6. Place the kebabs on the grill pan and grill them for 15 minutes turning frequently. Serve immediately.

TO DRINK

A soft full white wine would match these lovely  mediterranean flavours: try a white Rhône or New World Chardonnay.

RECIPE INFORMATION

RECIPE SERVES 4

Preparation - **15 minutes**
Cooking - **15 minutes**

AVERAGE VALUES PER PORTION
Calories - 185 kcals
Protein - 27g
Carbohydrate - 7g
Fat - 5g

COOK'S TIPS

Seafood does not keep, so buy the fish the day you intend to cook the kebabs.

Unsoaked scallops will not go rubbery when cooked - make this special request to your fishmonger.

FISH KEBABS

SALMON STEAKS WITH A HERB SAUCE

Fresh herbs and lemon make a light sauce which brings out the flavour of the salmon.

Salmon steaks	*4 (approx. 175g)*
Butter	*20g*
Plain flour	*20g*
Semi-skimmed milk	*300ml*
Wensleydale cheese	*120g, grated*
Fresh chervil	*1 tablespoon, finely chopped, plus sprigs to decorate*
Fresh chives	*8 blades, snipped*
Fresh parsley	*2 tablespoons, finely chopped*
Lemon	*1, zest and 1 tablespoon juice*
Rocket leaves	*to accompany*

METHOD

1. Grill the salmon steaks on a lined grill pan on a medium heat for 4 minutes each side. Turn off the heat but keep the steaks under the grill so they continue to cook and keep warm.

2. In a saucepan melt the butter and add the flour. Mix to a paste using 6 tablespoons of the milk. Whisking the mixture carefully, add the remaining milk and slowly bring to the boil. As the sauce thickens, whisk so there are no lumps.

3. Add the cheese and stir until melted. Fold in the herbs, turn off the heat, add the lemon zest and juice and stir.

4. Place each salmon steak on 4-6 rocket leaves. Drizzle the sauce over the fish, decorate with sprigs of chervil and serve immediately.

TO DRINK	RECIPE INFORMATION	COOK'S TIPS
To complement both the salmon and chervil in this dish, enjoy a chilled white wine such as a New Zealand Sauvignon Blanc.	RECIPE SERVES 4 Preparation - **10 minutes** Cooking - **15 minutes** AVERAGE VALUES PER PORTION Calories - 475 kcals Protein - 46g Carbohydrate - 7g Fat - 30g	If the sauce becomes lumpy it can be simply rectified by pouring it into a blender (or electric whisk) for a minute until smooth. Use 1 tsp of dried chervil if you are unable to get fresh.

SALMON STEAKS WITH A HERB SAUCE

MUSSELS IN CREAM

A creamy variation of moules à la marinière.

Butter	*15g*
Shallots	*2, finely chopped*
Celery	*50g, finely chopped*
Garlic cloves	*4, crushed*
White wine	*120ml*
Fresh mussels	*1.5kg, cleaned and ready prepared*
Fresh parsley	*3 tablespoons*
Fresh chives	*3 blades, snipped*
Single cream	*100ml*
Black pepper	*to season*

METHOD

1. Put the butter, shallots, celery, garlic and wine into
a very large saucepan and bring to the boil.

2. Add the mussels and 1 tablespoon of the parsley.
Cover the pan and cook on a high heat for about 5 minutes,
stirring well halfway through.
Take the lid off the pan and turn the heat to a low setting.

3. Add the remaining herbs, cream and black pepper
and fold into the mussels.
Cook for a further 2 minutes and serve.

TO DRINK

With a French classic such
as moules, there's no better
accompaniment than
a chilled French
cider.

RECIPE INFORMATION

RECIPE SERVES 4

Preparation - **10 minutes**
Cooking - **10 minutes**

AVERAGE VALUES PER PORTION
Calories - 205 kcals
Protein - 21g
Carbohydrate - 3g
Fat - 11g

COOK'S TIP

Always buy live mussels.
You can check this
by tapping their shells -
they should snap shut.
Discard any that
do not close or
have cracked shells.

MUSSELS IN CREAM

GRILLED TROUT WITH WATERCRESS SAUCE

A good farmhouse Lancashire, blended with fresh watercress makes an excellent partner with plump, juicy trout.

Watercress	*150g*
Crumbly Lancashire cheese	*90g*
Crème fraîche	*4 tablespoons*
Honey	*2 teaspoons*
Trout	*4, gutted and washed*
Sprigs of watercress	*to decorate*

METHOD

1. Chop the watercress and Lancashire cheese and add the crème fraîche. Place the ingredients in a blender and add the honey. Blend until smooth and then refrigerate.

2. Meanwhile wash the trout thoroughly with particular attention to the inner cavity of the fish and pat dry with kitchen paper.

3. Heat the grill on a medium setting.

4. Place the trout on a foil lined tray and grill for 6 minutes on each side.

5. Carefully place 1 tablespoon of the watercress sauce into the cavity of each trout. Put the remaining sauce into a serving bowl and set aside.

6. Grill the trout for 2 minutes, decorate with sprigs of watercress and serve with the remaining sauce.

TO DRINK	RECIPE INFORMATION	COOK'S TIP
Cheese and watercress give this dish an added 'bite'. Match with a crisp dry white such as Muscadet de Sèvre et Maine sur lie.	RECIPE SERVES 4 Preparation - **10 minutes** Cooking - **14 minutes** AVERAGE VALUES PER PORTION Calories - 575 kcals Protein - 7g Carbohydrate - 3g Fat - 13g	Be sure to keep the fish a good 10 cm *(4 inch)* from the grill. This will prevent the skin charring before the flesh is cooked.

GRILLED TROUT WITH WATERCRESS SAUCE

GARLIC AND CHILLI PRAWNS

A spicy variation on the classic garlic prawns recipe - this looks impressive.

Raw tiger prawns	*250g*
Garlic cloves	*5, sliced*
Sweet chilli sauce	*½ teaspoon*
Butter	*30g*
Olive oil	*2 tablespoons*
Black pepper	*to season*
Lemon	*2 tablespoons juice,* *1 tablespoon zest*

METHOD

1. Toss the tiger prawns in the garlic and chilli sauce.
Set aside for 15 minutes.

2. Melt the butter and the olive oil in a wok.

3. Stir fry the prawns for 3 minutes on a high heat
and season with the pepper.

4. Add the lemon juice and zest.
Cook for a further 3 minutes
and serve.

TO DRINK

The big flavours of this
dish require a big
white wine such as a
Semillon from Australia.

RECIPE INFORMATION

RECIPE SERVES 4

Preparation - **15 minutes**
Cooking - **7 minutes**

AVERAGE VALUES PER PORTION
Calories - 175 kcals
Protein - 11g
Carbohydrate - 2g
Fat - 14g

COOK'S TIP

You may have to order
the raw tiger prawns from
the supermarket or fish
shop. Often they can be
bought frozen - make sure
they are thoroughly
defrosted before use.

GARLIC AND CHILLI PRAWNS

BAKED HADDOCK IN CRÈME FRAÎCHE

A creamy alternative way of serving smoked haddock,
with extra flavour provided by spring onions and plenty of fresh chives.

Butter *15g*

Milk *6 tablespoons*

Smoked haddock *4 medium fillets*

Spring onions *6, chopped*

Crème fraîche *250ml*

Fresh chives *8 blades, snipped*

METHOD

1. Preheat the oven to 190°C.

2. Melt the butter, add the milk and pour into a baking dish, swirling the milk around to cover the base.

3. Cut the haddock fillets in half and place in the dish.

4. Mix the spring onions, crème fraîche and chives together and spoon over the haddock.

5. Cover the dish with foil and bake for 20-25 minutes.

TO DRINK

This dish needs a fuller flavoured, oaky white wine. Try an Australian barrel-fermented Semillon or Chardonnay.

RECIPE INFORMATION

RECIPE SERVES 4

Preparation - **10 minutes**
Cooking - **25 minutes**

AVERAGE VALUES PER PORTION
Calories - 500 kcals
Protein - 32g
Carbohydrate - 5g
Fat - 38g

COOK'S TIP

If you wish, use smoked cod instead of haddock. The colour of the fish will vary according to how the fish has been smoked and if colouring has been used to 'enhance' the fish.

BAKED HADDOCK IN CRÈME FRAÎCHE

ANCHOVY AND TOMATO MACARONI

A classic Italian combination of ripe plump tomatoes, olive oil and anchovies.

Anchovies	*30g, drained*
Ripe tomatoes	*250g*
Olives	*75g, pitted*
Olive oil	*2 teaspoons*
Macaroni	*300g*
Capers	*2 teaspoons*
Black pepper	*to season*

METHOD

1. Finely chop the anchovies, tomatoes and olives.
   Mix with the olive oil and set to one side.

2. Cook the macaroni according to the instructions on the packet.
   Drain and place back in the saucepan.

3. Add the anchovy mixture to the pasta and stir
   on a medium heat for 2 minutes.

4. Sprinkle the capers over the dish and season
   with plenty of black pepper.
   Spoon the pasta into a warmed serving bowl and serve.

TO DRINK

A light Spanish red wine goes superbly with this strongly flavoured dish. Otherwise a chilled dry rosé makes a good accompaniment.

RECIPE INFORMATION

RECIPE SERVES 4

Preparation - **5 minutes**
Cooking - **20 minutes**

AVERAGE VALUES PER PORTION
Calories - 345 kcals
Protein - 13g
Carbohydrate - 61g
Fat - 7g

COOK'S TIPS

Since anchovies are salty, there is no need to season the dish with salt.

Use very ripe fresh tomatoes to create a flavoursome dish.

Anchovy and Tomato Macaroni

PAN FRIED SCALLOPS IN GINGER, LIME AND CHILLI

A very special dish, 3 scallops per serving is enough as this is a very rich dish.

Ginger purée	*1 tablespoon*
Garlic clove	*1, crushed*
Chilli purée	*1 teaspoon*
Fresh lime	*6 tablespoons juice*
Sunflower oil	*2 tablespoons*
Fresh scallops	*12, large*
Peeled prawns	*100g, rinsed*
Butter	*25g*
Leeks	*2, peeled, washed and sliced*
Flat leaf parsley	*a handful, roughly chopped*

METHOD

1. Mix the ginger, garlic, chilli, lime juice and oil in a bowl.
   Add the scallops and prawns.

2. Heat the butter in a wok or large frying pan and add the leeks.
   Cook for 3 minutes.

3. Turn down the heat and carefully add the scallops and prawns to the pan
   with the juices. Gently sauté for 10 minutes turning the scallops
   every so often to ensure they are evenly cooked.

4. Scatter the parsley over the dish. Stir and cook for another minute,
   then serve.

TO DRINK

The clean fresh flavours
of New Zealand
Chardonnay would work
well with this flavoursome
combination.

RECIPE INFORMATION

RECIPE SERVES 4

Preparation - **10 minutes**
Cooking - **15 minutes**

AVERAGE VALUES PER PORTION
Calories - 210 kcals
Protein - 18g
Carbohydrate - 6g
Fat - 13g

COOK'S TIP

Use fresh, shelled or
defrosted prawns of
your choice.

PAN FRIED SCALLOPS IN GINGER, LIME AND CHILLI

AROMATIC COD

A creamy yet spiced flavour makes this a delicious alternative way of serving cod.

Oil	*1 teaspoon*
Onions	*2, thinly sliced*
Cod steaks	*4*
Yogurt	*250g*
Fresh parsley	*4 tablespoons, chopped*
Cayenne pepper	*½ teaspoon*
Cinnamon	*2 teaspoons*
Cumin	*2 teaspoons*
Selection of fresh vegetables	*to serve*

METHOD

1. Brush a serving dish with the oil and sprinkle half the onions over the base of the dish.

2. Clean the cod steaks under cold water and then place them over the onions.

3. Preheat the oven to 200°C. Meanwhile mix the yogurt, parsley, cayenne pepper, cinnamon and cumin with the remaining onions. Spoon over the fish. Leave for 10 minutes to allow the flavours to develop.

4. Cover the fish with baking foil and bake for 20 minutes. Remove the foil and bake for a further 6 minutes. Serve hot with a selection of fresh vegetables.

TO DRINK

An ice cold lager goes well with this spicy dish. Alternatively a chilled unoaked white wine such as a French or Italian Chardonnay.

RECIPE INFORMATION

RECIPE SERVES 4

Preparation - **15 minutes**
Cooking - **26 minutes**

AVERAGE VALUES PER PORTION
Calories - 210 kcals
Protein - 35g
Carbohydrate - 10g
Fat - 3g

COOK'S TIP

Cayenne pepper is extremely hot, not to be confused with paprika, so use sparingly. This pungent spice comprises the finely ground flesh and seeds of dried red peppers. It is the seeds that make it so fiery.

AROMATIC COD

LING FILLETS WITH PARSLEY AND TOMATO PESTO

A simple dish which sums up 'everyday specials' - a medley of summer flavours which make baked fish so much more interesting.

PESTO

Fresh parsley *1 large handful*

Sundried tomatoes in oil *5, plus 1 tablespoon oil*

Pine kernels *4 tablespoons*

Garlic clove *1, chopped*

Extra virgin olive oil *120ml*

Ling fillets *4*

METHOD

1. Blend the pesto ingredients in a food processor. Spoon into a bowl, set to one side and leave for 5 minutes to allow the flavours to develop. Meanwhile preheat the oven to 200°C.

2. Rinse the fillets and dry with absorbent kitchen paper.

3. Line an ovenproof tray with kitchen foil, sufficient to wrap the fish into a parcel.

4. Place the fish on the foil and smear generously with the pesto sauce, allowing it to drizzle down the sides of the fish.
Seal the foil keeping a small hole in the centre, about 5 cm *(2 inch)*.
Bake in the oven for 30-35 minutes.

TO DRINK

A clean, crisp dry white that will not overpower the fish such as Entre Deux Mers or other dry white Bordeaux.

RECIPE INFORMATION

RECIPE SERVES 4

Preparation - **10 minutes**
Cooking - **35 minutes**

AVERAGE VALUES PER PORTION
Calories - 460 kcals
Protein - 31g
Carbohydrate - 4g
Fat - 34g

COOK'S TIPS

This pesto will keep in the fridge for about a week and is superb on pizzas or mixed into hot pasta.

Cod, haddock or hoki can be used for this recipe as a substitute.

LING FILLETS WITH PARSLEY AND TOMATO PESTO

SPANISH CHICKEN

The ingredient list may seem long but this rustic, rich stew is bursting with Mediterranean flavours.

Flour	*2 tablespoons*
Dried mixed herbs	*1 tablespoon*
Boneless chicken thighs	*8*
Oil	*2 tablespoons*
Butter	*25g*
Spanish onions	*2, sliced into rings*
Garlic cloves	*3, sliced*
Chorizo sausage	*150g, sliced*
Red pepper	*1, sliced into rings*
Chopped tomatoes	*1 small tin (230g)*
Chicken stock	*250ml*
Red wine	*100ml*
Fresh thyme	*to decorate*

METHOD

1. Mix the flour with the herbs and coat the chicken thighs.

2. Heat the oil and butter in a heavy based casserole and brown the meat. Take out of the pan and then sauté the onions and garlic in the juices for 2 minutes.

3. Turn up the heat, add the sausage and pepper and fry for 2 minutes. Add the chicken back to the pan and add the tomatoes. Stir and add the stock. Once the liquid starts to bubble turn down to a simmer and add the wine.

4. Cover and cook on a low heat for 30 minutes. Decorate with thyme and serve.

TO DRINK

A rich Spanish red such as Toro would suit this flamboyant dish.

RECIPE INFORMATION

RECIPE SERVES 4

Preparation - **10 minutes**
Cooking - **30 minutes**

AVERAGE VALUES PER PORTION
Calories - 485 kcals
Protein - 35g
Carbohydrate - 13g
Fat - 31g

COOK'S TIP

Chorizo sausage is a highly seasoned pork sausage providing plenty of flavour, so there's no need to add extra seasoning to this dish.

Spanish Chicken

SWEET AND SOUR GAMMON WITH PEACHES

The sweetness of the peaches with the savoury gammon makes a delicious and different dish.

SAUCE

Rice wine vinegar	*4 tablespoons*
Tinned peaches	*500g, including juice*
Chilli sauce	*1 teaspoon*
Onion	*1 small, finely chopped*
Soy sauce	*4 tablespoons*
Sesame oil	*2 teaspoons*

Gammon steaks	*4*

METHOD

1. Combine all the sauce ingredients and blend in a food processor for about 10 seconds until slightly chunky, but well mixed. Set aside and leave for 10 minutes for the flavour to develop.

2. Grill the gammon steaks on a medium heat for 4 minutes on each side and remove to a plate but keep warm.

3. Place the sauce in a large pan and add the meat juices. Cook for 2 minutes. Cut the steaks in half and add to the pan, spooning the sauce over the gammon.

4. Cook for 2 minutes and serve straight away with your favourite vegetables.

TO DRINK

Slightly sweeter white wines are best with this dish. Try a German Riesling Spätlese or a Liebfraumilch.

RECIPE INFORMATION

RECIPE SERVES 4

Preparation - **10 minutes**
Cooking - **12 minutes**

AVERAGE VALUES PER PORTION
Calories - 385 kcals
Protein - 32g
Carbohydrate - 43g
Fat - 11g

COOK'S TIP

Gammon is naturally salty and is therefore excellent with a sweet sauce. Don't be tempted to add seasoning to the sauce.

SWEET AND SOUR GAMMON WITH PEACHES

TURKEY PILAFF

A superb array of colours and flavours.
This popular classic all-in-one dish will satisfy the most demanding appetites.

Hazelnut oil *3 tablespoons*	**Chicken stock** *700ml*
Shallots *250g, quartered*	**Broad beans** *100g, shelled*
Garlic cloves *2, slivered*	**Cooked turkey** *350g, sliced into strips*
Medium strength curry powder *1 tablespoon*	**Tinned apricots** *150g, quartered plus 3 tablespoons juice*
Mixed spice *2 teaspoons*	**Pine nuts** *2 tablespoons, toasted*
Long grain rice *225g*	**Fresh flat leaf parsley** *3 tablespoons, roughly chopped*

METHOD

1. Heat the oil in a casserole and add the shallots.
Cook for 3 minutes, add the garlic and spices
and continue to cook for 2 minutes.

2. Add the rice and stir well. Add the stock and bring to the boil.
Cover and simmer for 10 minutes, stirring occasionally.
If you are using fresh broad beans add them now.
If you are using frozen or tinned, add them after another 6 minutes.

3. When the rice has simmered for 16 minutes and you have added the beans,
add the turkey to the pilaff with the apricots and their juice.
Cover and cook for 10 minutes, stirring occasionally.

4. Take the dish off the heat and sprinkle with the pine nuts and parsley.

TO DRINK

A Californian, Australian
or Chilean Cabernet
Sauvignon red wine is
excellent
with this
turkey
recipe.

RECIPE INFORMATION
RECIPE SERVES 4
Preparation - **5 minutes**
Cooking - **30 minutes**

AVERAGE VALUES PER PORTION
Calories - 515 kcals
Protein - 33g
Carbohydrate - 64g
Fat - 4g

COOK'S TIP

If you can't bear the
thought of peeling shallots,
use 3 small English onions
(which have more flavour
than the larger varieties)
and cut them into
8 pieces each.

TURKEY PILAFF

PORK WITH APPLE AND SAGE

As the summer draws to a close, this recipe makes the most of an autumnal harvest of
English produce using apples, shallots, farmhouse cider and sage.

Butter	*30g*
Shallots	*3, peeled and very finely chopped*
Pork fillet	*300g, sliced*
Red apples	*2, cored and sliced into thin wedges*
Brown sugar	*1 tablespoon*
Fresh sage	*1 tablespoon, chopped plus extra sprigs to decorate*
Cider vinegar	*3 tablespoons*
Cider	*125ml*

METHOD

1. Heat the butter in a large pan and fry the shallots until transparent.

2. Add the pork fillet to the shallots and cook gently for about 3 minutes on each side.

3. Add the apples, sugar, sage, cider vinegar and cider. Stir and cook for 15 minutes on a gentle heat.

4. Season if necessary, decorate with the fresh sage and serve at once.

TO DRINK

To ring the changes try a chilled farmhouse English cider to bring out the apple in the recipe.

RECIPE INFORMATION

RECIPE SERVES 4

Preparation - **5 minutes**
Cooking - **20 minutes**

AVERAGE VALUES PER PORTION
Calories - 230 kcals
Protein - 16g
Carbohydrate - 14g
Fat - 12g

COOK'S TIP

This recipe works equally well with pork chops.

PORK WITH APPLE AND SAGE

LAMB COUSCOUS

A Moroccan classic - tender young lamb gently cooked with spiced couscous, herbs, tomatoes and a twist of lime.

Couscous	*150g*
Vegetable stock	*350ml*
Olive oil	*2 tablespoons*
Lamb	*400g, trimmed and cut into small cubes*
Onion	*1, diced*
Garlic cloves	*2, crushed*
Cumin seeds	*2 teaspoons*
Cinnamon	*1 teaspoon*
Chopped tomatoes	*1 small tin (approx. 220g)*
Raisins	*50g*
Fresh coriander	*1 handful, stems removed*
Lime	*1, cut into wedges*

METHOD

1. Prepare the couscous by rinsing it and then soaking it in the vegetable stock which should have just boiled. Fluff it up with a fork after about 5 minutes and set aside.

2. Heat the oil in a large pan and gently cook the lamb for 5 minutes, then add the onion and garlic. Stir well and add the spices. Cover and cook on a low heat for 5 minutes.

3. Add the tomatoes and their juice, the raisins and couscous. Season and cook covered for 8 minutes. Decorate with the coriander and lime wedges and serve whilst hot.

TO DRINK	RECIPE INFORMATION	COOK'S TIP
In North Africa, the accompaniment would be mint tea. But why not try a Greek or Lebanese red wine?	RECIPE SERVES 4 Preparation - **10 minutes** Cooking - **20 minutes** AVERAGE VALUES PER PORTION Calories - 550 kcals Protein - 19g Carbohydrate - 29g Fat - 40g	Couscous is a cereal processed from semolina with very little flavour - it is the texture that makes it so interesting.

Lamb Couscous

CALVES' LIVER WITH CARAMELISED ONIONS

A hearty classic - tender pink calves liver with sweet onions and traditional black pudding.

Onions	*2, sliced*
Brown sugar	*2 tablespoons*
Butter	*25g*
Flour	*2 tablespoons*
Black pepper	*to season*
Calves' liver	*4 thin slices (approx. 350g)*
Black pudding	*4-8 slices (according to size of the cut)*
Bacon rashers	*3, chopped*
Fresh parsley	*3 tablespoons, chopped*

METHOD

1. Preheat the oven to 170°C. Place the onion, sugar and butter in a frying pan and heat slowly, stirring occasionally. As the butter melts, turn up the heat and fry the onions for 2-3 minutes on high. When they are starting to turn golden, spoon them into an ovenproof dish and put in the oven.

2. Coat the calves' liver with the flour and black pepper.

3. Fry the black pudding in the pan until crisp on both sides. Pat with absorbent kitchen paper and keep hot with the onions.

4. Fry the bacon for 2 minutes and add the calves' liver. Cook on a medium heat for 2-3 minutes on each side. Sprinkle the parsley over the liver and turn off the heat.

5. Serve the liver on warmed plates with the black pudding and onions.

TO DRINK

This combination of liver and onion is extremely well suited to Australian Shiraz. Other rich red wines such as Médoc or Barolo are excellent.

RECIPE INFORMATION

RECIPE SERVES 4

Preparation - **10 minutes**
Cooking - **10 minutes**

AVERAGE VALUES PER PORTION
Calories - 415 kcals
Protein - 27g
Carbohydrate - 21g
Fat - 25g

COOK'S TIPS

Calves' liver only requires a couple of minutes to cook and should be slightly pink in the middle.

For a more economical dish use lamb's liver.

CALVES' LIVER WITH CARAMELISED ONIONS

TORTILLA PLATTER

A Mexican fiesta of flavours - a classic chilli con carne served on a bed of crisp tortillas and salad.

CHILLI SAUCE

Oil	*1 tablespoon*
Onion	*1, finely chopped*
Garlic cloves	*2, crushed*
Minced beef	*400g*
Tomato passata	*4 tablespoons*
Chilli sauce	*1 teaspoon*
Ground coriander	*2 teaspoons*
Kidney beans	*1 small tin (220g) drained*

OTHER INGREDIENTS

Iceberg lettuce	*½ shredded*
Tortilla chips	*1 large bag*
Cheddar cheese	*75g, grated*
Soured cream	*4 tablespoons*
Fresh coriander	*Large bunch, rinsed and trimmed to sprigs*

METHOD

1. Heat the oil in a large pan and fry the onion for 2 minutes then add the garlic. Cook for 1 minute then remove from the pan. Fry the beef on a medium setting in the pan juices for 6 minutes until starting to brown.

2. Add the onions back to the pan with the passata, chilli sauce and coriander. Cook on a medium heat for 10 minutes. Add the kidney beans and simmer.

3. Arrange the iceberg lettuce on a large platter and top with the tortilla chips and half the Cheddar cheese.

4. Spoon the chilli mixture over the tortillas. Sprinkle the remaining Cheddar over the chilli. Top with the soured cream and coriander sprigs and serve right away.

TO DRINK

A chilled Mexican lager with a wedge of lime is the obvious choice.

RECIPE INFORMATION

RECIPE SERVES 4

Preparation - **10 minutes**
Cooking - **20 minutes**

AVERAGE VALUES PER PORTION
Calories - 580 kcals
Protein - 33g
Carbohydrate - 32g
Fat - 37g

COOK'S TIP

Don't leave this dish standing or the tortilla chips will go soggy.

TORTILLA PLATTER

BACON BRUSSELS SPROUTS

*Forget that soggy mush from your school-days and enjoy this highly nutritious dish -
a superb extra special TV dinner.*

Brussels sprouts	*450g, peeled and washed*
Baby carrots	*350g, scrubbed and halved lengthways*
Butter	*15g*
Onion	*1 large, chopped*
Bacon	*6 rashers, sliced*
Garlic cloves	*2, sliced*
White wine vinegar	*90ml*
Honey	*1 tablespoon*
Fresh parsley	*1 tablespoon, chopped*

METHOD

1. Steam the Brussels sprouts and carrots until *al dente* (about 10 minutes).
Drain and rinse under cold water.

2. Melt the butter in a frying pan and fry the onion until soft.
Add the bacon and cook for 3 minutes until starting to crisp.
Add the garlic, Brussels sprouts and carrots
and cook for 2 minutes, stirring.

3. Add the vinegar, honey and half the parsley.
Cook for 2 minutes keeping the heat high.

4. Spoon into a warmed serving dish, sprinkle with the
remaining parsley and serve.

TO DRINK

We sampled a chilled premium quality Bramley apple juice which made a perfect partner to this dish.

RECIPE INFORMATION

RECIPE SERVES 4

Preparation - **10 minutes**
Cooking - **20 minutes**

AVERAGE VALUES PER PORTION
Calories - 245 kcals
Protein - 11g
Carbohydrate - 14g
Fat - 16g

COOK'S TIP

Plunging the steamed vegetables into cold water will preserve their colour and stop the Brussels sprouts going yellow.

BACON BRUSSELS SPROUTS

CHICKEN LIVER SALAD

A rich colourful array of ingredients create a simple yet special dish.

Butter	*25g*
Garlic cloves	*2, crushed*
Chicken livers	*300g, sliced*
Mixed salad leaves	*250g, washed*
Cherry tomatoes	*12, washed*
Extra virgin olive oil	*2 tablespoons*
Wholegrain mustard	*2 teaspoons*
Balsamic vinegar	*2 tablespoons*

METHOD

1. Melt the butter in a frying pan and add the garlic.
Stir and add the chicken livers.
Cook on a medium heat for 5 minutes.

2. Meanwhile, toss the salad leaves and tomatoes in
the olive oil and arrange on a large platter.

3. Add the wholegrain mustard to the
chicken livers and stir.

4. Turn up the heat and add the balsamic vinegar.
Cook for 2 minutes then spoon over the
salad platter and serve straight away.

TO DRINK

The strong flavour of chicken liver requires a robust red wine such as Barolo or Barbaresco.

RECIPE INFORMATION

RECIPE SERVES 4

Preparation - **10 minutes**
Cooking - **8 minutes**

AVERAGE VALUES PER PORTION
Calories - 235 kcals
Protein - 16g
Carbohydrate - 4g
Fat - 17g

COOK'S TIP

Liver becomes very tough when overcooked, which is easy to do with small chicken livers. Therefore slightly undercook it and let the residual heat finish the cooking for you.

CHICKEN LIVER SALAD

SHROPSHIRE BLUE AND PORT SIRLOIN STEAKS

*This is a delightfully rich, extravagant dish - excellent for celebrations
and you won't spend all evening in the kitchen preparing and clearing up!*

Shropshire Blue cheese *120g, crumbled*

Mascarpone cheese *6 tablespoons*

Port *3 tablespoons*

Sirloin steaks *4*

Sunflower oil *1 tablespoon*

Pine nuts *2 tablespoons*

Black pepper *to season*

Fresh parsley *3 tablespoons, roughly chopped, to garnish*

METHOD

1. Blend the cheeses and port in a food processor or blender.
Spoon into a bowl and cover.

2. Brush the steaks with the oil and grill to your desired depth of cooking
(i.e. 3 minutes each side for rare).
Warm the pine nuts on a baking sheet under the grill at the same time.

3. Place the cheese mixture into a pan and heat until melted and bubbling.
Add the pine nuts, stir and season with the black pepper.

4. Add the steaks to the pan and cook for 1½ minutes.
Garnish with the parsley and serve with a selection of
traditional vegetables and lightly roasted potatoes in their skins.

TO DRINK

Red wines are excellent with
the ingredients of this dish -
If you feel extravagant go
for a Châteauneuf du Pape or
Barolo, alternatively try a
good Australian Shiraz.

RECIPE INFORMATION

RECIPE SERVES 4

Preparation - **10 minutes**
Cooking - **10 minutes**

AVERAGE VALUES PER PORTION
Calories - 880 kcals
Protein - 45g
Carbohydrate - 4g
Fat - 74g

COOK'S TIPS

Be careful not to heat the
cheese mixture too quickly.
Stir the mixture continually
until it has evenly melted.

Use Stilton as an
alternative to
Shropshire Blue.

SHROPSHIRE BLUE AND PORT SIRLOIN STEAKS

ROAST POUSSIN WITH LEMON, GARLIC AND HERBS

This zesty dish is packed full of flavours and looks like the creation of a masterchef.
Bon appetit!

Sunflower oil	*8 tablespoons*
Fresh lemon juice	*4 tablespoons*
Fresh thyme	*3 tablespoons, chopped plus sprigs to decorate*
Fresh oregano	*2 tablespoons, chopped*
Fresh rosemary	*1 handful, divided into small sprigs*
Poussin	*4, ready prepared*
Garlic cloves	*12, left whole, but slightly squashed*
Lemons	*2, halved*
Black peppercorns	*1 teaspoon, crushed rather than ground*

METHOD

1. Place the poussin in a roasting dish. Combine the oil, juice and herbs and pour over the poussin.
Set to one side whilst you preheat the oven to 200°C.

2. Place the garlic cloves with the poussin and roast them for 15 minutes.

3. Baste the birds with the pan juices, slightly squeeze the lemon halves over them and then add them to the pan. Add the pepper, place the birds back in the oven and roast for a further 15-20 minutes.

4. Baste with the juices once more, decorate with sprigs of thyme and serve with crisp roast potatoes and a green salad.

TO DRINK

A refreshing dry Vinho Verde from Northern Portugal would allow the delicate flavour of the poussin to come through.

RECIPE INFORMATION

RECIPE SERVES 4
Preparation - **5 minutes**
Cooking - **35 minutes**

AVERAGE VALUES PER PORTION
Calories - 655 kcals
Protein - 83g
Carbohydrate - 4g
Fat - 34g

COOK'S TIP

Poussin are much more widely available now, even from larger supermarkets. Alternatively use chicken quarters.

ROAST POUSSIN WITH LEMON, GARLIC AND HERBS

TURKEY MARSALA

A speedy dish using the best Italian Marsala wine.

Turkey breast steaks	*450g, skinned*
Flour	*2 tablespoons*
Olive oil	*1 tablespoon*
Butter	*25g*
Marsala wine	*100ml*
Double cream	*75ml*
Black pepper	*to season*

METHOD

1. Flatten the turkey steaks into thin escalopes and dust with flour.

2. Heat the oil and butter in a frying pan and add the turkey.

3. Cook the turkey for 4 minutes on each side and remove to a warmed plate, keeping the juices in the pan.

4. Turn up the heat and pour the Marsala wine into the pan. Stir vigorously with the pan juices, then add the turkey back to the pan.

5. Turn the heat down to low and add the cream and pepper. Cook for another minute and serve.

TO DRINK

For this subtle dish, a chilled white wine such as Burgundy or Chablis go well.

RECIPE INFORMATION

RECIPE SERVES 4

Preparation - **5 minutes**
Cooking - **10 minutes**

AVERAGE VALUES PER PORTION
Calories - 320 kcals
Protein - 27g
Carbohydrate - 4g
Fat - 19g

COOK'S TIP

Flatten the turkey breasts on a board using a rolling pin, applying a gentle pressure to the meat.

TURKEY MARSALA

CHICKEN HOTPOT WITH DUMPLINGS

Light fluffy dumplings with the delicate flavour of caraway adorn this hearty stew.

FOR THE HOTPOT	FOR THE DUMPLINGS
Olive oil *2 tablespoons*	**Self raising flour** *100g*
Chicken goujons *10 (about 350g)*	**Suet** *50g*
Onion *1, sliced*	**Egg** *1, beaten*
Baby button mushrooms *150g, wiped and left whole*	**Fresh parsley** *3 tablespoons, chopped*
Celery *2 sticks, sliced*	**Caraway seeds** *1 heaped teaspoon*
Ready-made vegetable pasta sauce *1 jar (approx. 400g)*	**Black pepper** *to season*
Red wine *100ml*	

METHOD

1. Heat the oil in a large casserole and gently fry the chicken for 3 minutes. Add the onion, mushrooms and celery and cook for a further 3 minutes.

2. Add the pasta sauce and red wine. Cover and simmer whilst you make the dumplings. Preheat the oven to 200°C.

3. Make the dumplings by combining all the ingredients in a food processor or bowl, to form a dough. From this mixture shape 8 dumplings, similar in size to golf balls.

4. Stir the hotpot then carefully place the dumplings on the top, cover and bake for 26 minutes, removing the casserole lid for the last 3 minutes of cooking.

TO DRINK	RECIPE INFORMATION	COOK'S TIP
This warming, savoury dish would be delicious with a good red Burgundy.	RECIPE SERVES 4 Preparation - **15 minutes** Cooking - **30 minutes** AVERAGE VALUES PER PORTION Calories - 465 kcals Protein - 26g Carbohydrate - 33g Fat - 25g	If you can't buy goujons, buy skinless, boneless chicken thighs and cut them into strips.

CHICKEN HOTPOT WITH DUMPLINGS

AROMATIC, SPICY COCONUT LAMB

A cocktail of flavours created with these spices and sweet taste of coconut and fresh mint.

Fresh ginger *4 tablespoons, peeled and chopped*

Garlic cloves *6, crushed*

Shallots *3, diced*

Cardamom pods *8, seeds only*

Ground cloves *½ teaspoon*

Cumin seeds, cinnamon & turmeric *1 tablespoon of each*

Mustard seeds *2 teaspoons*

Green chillies *2, deseeded and sliced*

Sunflower oil *3 tablespoons*

Lamb fillet *675g, trimmed and cubed*

Coconut cream *1 sachet or 50g block*

Water *60ml*

Fresh mint *3 tablespoons, chopped*

METHOD

1. Blend the ginger, garlic, shallots, spices, chillies and sunflower oil in a food processor until smooth.

2. Spoon over the cubed lamb in a casserole. Preheat the oven to 190°C.

3. Chop the coconut cream and add to the dish with the water.

4. Cover and bake in the oven for 40 minutes, stirring 3 or 4 times during this time.

5. Take out of the oven and stir in the fresh mint. Serve at once.

TO DRINK

A premium 'ice' lager goes well with this dish. For a wine, try an aromatic, spicy white Gewurztraminer d' Alsace.

RECIPE INFORMATION

RECIPE SERVES 4

Preparation - **5 minutes**
Cooking - **40 minutes**

AVERAGE VALUES PER PORTION
Calories - 640 kcals
Protein - 49g
Carbohydrate - 7g
Fat - 46g

COOK'S TIP

To remove the seeds from a cardamom pod, crush them slightly with a pestle and mortar or the side of a knife blade. Remove the seeds with your fingers.

AROMATIC, SPICY COCONUT LAMB

CHICKEN PÖRKÖLT

A Hungarian classic - paprika providing the stunning colour and flavour.

Lard (or butter) *25g*	
Boneless chicken thighs *8, skinned*	
Onions *2, medium sliced*	
Garlic cloves *2, crushed*	
Red pepper *1, diced*	
Chestnut mushrooms *250g, peeled and sliced*	
Paprika *2 heaped tablespoons*	
Chicken stock *200ml*	
Soured cream *60ml*	

METHOD

1. Melt the lard in a heavy based casserole and gently brown the chicken thighs.

2. Add the onions and cook until transparent.

3. Add the garlic, pepper and mushrooms and stir, then add the paprika.

4. Stir in the chicken stock and heat until bubbling.
Cover and simmer for 25 minutes, stirring occasionally.

5. Just before serving, swirl the soured cream into the dish.
Add another dust of paprika and serve with
boiled potatoes or rice.

TO DRINK

A Hungarian red wine,
with Merlot the best
choice.

RECIPE INFORMATION

RECIPE SERVES 4

Preparation - **10 minutes**
Cooking - **25 minutes**

AVERAGE VALUES PER PORTION
Calories - 405 kcals
Protein - 48g
Carbohydrate - 10g
Fat - 20g

COOK'S TIP

It is important to remove
the dish from the heat
before adding the
soured cream.
If the cream is
overheated it separates.

Chicken Pörkölt

TARRAGON TURKEY

Fresh tarragon with crushed peppercorns are the key to this flavoursome dish.
Don't attempt to make this recipe with dried herbs.

Turkey breast	*2 large, skinned*
Sunflower oil	*3 tablespoons*
Fresh tarragon	*4 tablespoons roughly chopped, plus 3 sprigs for garnish*
Crushed peppercorns	*½ teaspoon*
White wine	*75ml*

METHOD

1. Slice the turkey into strips and place in a shallow dish with the oil. Stir the tarragon into the turkey. Add the pepper and leave to marinate for 15-20 minutes.

2. Heat a large frying pan and add the turkey with the marinade. Cook for 4 minutes so that the meat is brown all over.

3. Add the wine and continue to cook for 3-4 minutes until the liquid has reduced.

4. Decorate with the extra tarragon and serve at once.

TO DRINK

Chilean and South African Sauvignon Blancs go best with tarragon. Otherwise try an Italian Frascati.

RECIPE INFORMATION

RECIPE SERVES 4

Preparation - **20 minutes**
Cooking - **8 minutes**

AVERAGE VALUES PER PORTION
Calories - 275 kcals
Protein - 38g
Carbohydrate - 0.5g
Fat - 12g

COOK'S TIP

Keep the heat on a medium setting so that the tarragon does not scorch.
If the tarragon starts to burn, the turkey is cooking too fast as well.

TARRAGON TURKEY

PORK WITH PRUNES

A rich and fruity sauce adds flavour and interest to the pork in this dish.

Ready-to-eat stoned prunes	*150g*
Red wine	*250ml*
Olive oil	*2 tablespoons*
Pork chops	*4*
Redcurrant jelly	*1 tablespoon*
Cornflour	*2 teaspoons in 3 tablespoons of cold water*
Double cream	*2 tablespoons*

METHOD

1. Place the prunes in a bowl and add the wine. Put to one side.

2. Heat the oil in a frying pan and cook the pork chops on a medium-hot heat for 5 minutes each side, until brown.

3. Add the redcurrant jelly and cornflour to the pan and stir. Add the prunes with the wine.

4. Leave to simmer for 20 minutes, stirring occasionally, allowing the liquid to reduce.

5. Take off the heat, if necessary season and stir in the cream. Serve at once.

TO DRINK

A Vouvray Demi-sec goes excellently with the sweet prunes and cream in this dish.

RECIPE INFORMATION

RECIPE SERVES 4

Preparation - **5 minutes**
Cooking - **35 minutes**

AVERAGE VALUES PER PORTION
Calories - 640 kcals
Protein - 22g
Carbohydrate - 19g
Fat - 49g

COOK'S TIP

When buying pork chops, look for white fat around the meat and chops that are about 2.5 cm *(1 inch)* thick. This ensures that the chops remain succulent.

PRUNES WITH PORK

FRIDAY NIGHT FEAST

This is the picnic you enjoy in the kitchen on a Friday night,
when you don't want loads of washing up, but want a good start to the weekend!

Somerset brie	*275g*
Continental ham	*12 slices*
Foccacia bread	*1 loaf*
Artichoke pieces in oil	*1 jar (approx. 300g), drained*
Antipasto vegetables	*1 jar (approx. 280g), drained*
Mixed olives	*50g*
Cherry tomatoes	*100g, washed*
Fresh figs	*4, quartered*
Mixed salad	*to accompany*

METHOD

1. Remove the cheese and ham from the fridge and bring up to room temperature (about 15 minutes).

2. Preheat the oven to 160°C. Place the bread in the oven to warm through for about 5 minutes.

3. Arrange the remaining ingredients on a large platter or alternatively on individual plates.

4. Serve with the warm bread and the mixed salad.

TO DRINK

Relax! The many different flavours here mean you can just have whatever you fancy - or whatever you've got!

RECIPE INFORMATION

RECIPE SERVES 4

Preparation - **15 minutes**
Cooking - **5 minutes**

AVERAGE VALUES PER PORTION
Calories - 690 kcals
Protein - 34g
Carbohydrate - 48g
Fat - 41g

COOK'S TIP

Reserve the oil from the artichoke hearts to make a fragrant and fresh salad dressing.

FRIDAY NIGHT FEAST

Sizzling Beef

Everyone's favourite at the local Chinese, this is so simple to make at home.

Worcester sauce	*1 tablespoon*
Soy sauce	*2 tablespoons*
Tomato purée	*1 tablespoon*
Sherry vinegar	*1 tablespoon*
Honey	*1 tablespoon*
Sesame oil	*2 teaspoons*
Sunflower oil	*2 teaspoons*
Rump steak	*650g, sliced into strips*
Sesame seeds	*2 tablespoons*
Spring onions	*6, trimmed and roughly chopped*
Beansprouts and Chinese noodles	*to serve*

METHOD

1. Mix the Worcester sauce with the soy sauce, tomato purée, sherry vinegar and honey. Leave for about 10 minutes to allow the flavours to develop.

2. Heat the oils in a wok and stir fry the steak on a high heat. After 1 minute add the sesame seeds and the sauce.

3. Add the spring onions and cook for 2 minutes then serve on a bed of beansprouts and Chinese noodles.

TO DRINK

For the oriental touch, try some Saki wine.

Since this isn't always easy to find try a pot of freshly brewed Jasmine tea.

RECIPE INFORMATION

RECIPE SERVES 4

Preparation - **10 minutes**
Cooking - **5 minutes**

AVERAGE VALUES PER PORTION
Calories - 410 kcals
Protein - 32g
Carbohydrate - 6g
Fat - 28g

COOK'S TIP

A wok is essential for this dish not because of the high heat that is needed but because you need enough room in your wok to continually toss the ingredients.

SIZZLING BEEF

CELERIAC BAKE WITH SMOKED TURKEY

Celeriac and potatoes go well together - the addition of the smoked turkey makes a wholesome dish.
Our picture shows a single portion.

Old potatoes	*400g, peeled*
Celeriac	*400g, peeled*
Onion	*1, peeled*
Seasoning	
Crème fraîche	*300ml*
Smoked turkey breast	*150g*
Cheshire cheese	*100g, grated*

METHOD

1. Preheat the oven to 210°C.

2. Using a grater attachment for the food processor,
   grate all the vegetables.

3. Place the vegetables into a large bowl, season and stir in the crème fraîche.

4. Slice the smoked turkey into strips and stir into the mixture.
   Stir in half the cheese.

5. Spoon the mixture into a deep, greased, ovenproof serving dish.
   Scatter the remaining cheese over the top of the dish.
   Cover with foil and bake for 35 minutes.
   Remove the foil and bake for another 3 minutes then serve.

TO DRINK

Celeriac tastes of a
combination of celery
and parsley.

Dry white wines
are best with
these flavours - try
a white Rioja

RECIPE INFORMATION

RECIPE SERVES 4

Preparation - **7 minutes**
Cooking - **38 minutes**

AVERAGE VALUES PER PORTION
Calories - 525 kcals
Protein - 19g
Carbohydrate - 28g
Fat - 38g

COOK'S TIP

After peeling the celeriac
(and before grating it)
soak it in cold water mixed
with a little lemon juice.
This prevents
discolouration but doesn't
interfere with the flavour.

Celeriac Bake with Smoked Turkey

Spiced Sausage and Bean Hotpot

An economical everyday dish popular with all the family.

Sunflower oil	*2 tablespoons*
Premium pork chipolatas	*8*
Onion	*1, sliced*
Pepperoni sausage	*80g, chopped*
Tomato purée	*1 tablespoon*
Chopped tomatoes	*1 large tin (400g)*
Cumin seeds	*2 teaspoons*
Dried coriander	*2 teaspoons*
Worcester sauce	*1 tablespoon*
Cannellini beans	*1 large tin (390g), drained*

METHOD

1. Heat the oil in a casserole. Add the chipolatas to the pan and cook for 10 minutes until brown.

2. Add the onion and cook for 3 minutes.
Add the pepperoni, tomato purée, tomatoes and spices.
Cover and cook for 10 minutes on a simmer.

3. Add the Worcester sauce and beans.
Stir well, then cover and simmer for 10 minutes.
Serve with mashed potatoes.

TO DRINK

Choose a robust, red wine from Portugal or the South of France - better still a traditional Mexican or Spanish lager, ice cold.

RECIPE INFORMATION

RECIPE SERVES 4

Preparation - **5 minutes**
Cooking - **33 minutes**

AVERAGE VALUES PER PORTION
Calories - 660 kcals
Protein - 24g
Carbohydrate - 31g
Fat - 49g

COOK'S TIP

Any pepperoni can be used but don't add too much seasoning, as pepperoni tends to be very salty.

SPICED SAUSAGE AND BEAN HOTPOT

Pan Fried Venison with Apricots

*Rich gamy venison and smoky bacon are offset by fruity apricots
resulting in a warming delectable dish.*

Dried apricots	*110g, halved*
Sherry	*60ml*
Venison	*450g, cubed*
Flour	*2 tablespoons*
Sunflower oil	*2 tablespoons*
Bacon rashers	*3, finely chopped*
Shallots	*3, diced*
Water	*75ml*

METHOD

1. Soak the apricots in the sherry for at least 20 minutes.

2. Meanwhile dust the meat with the flour.

3. Heat the oil in a frying pan on a low heat and add the venison.
   Cook gently for 4 minutes.

4. Add the bacon and the shallots, stir and then add the water.
   Cover and cook for 5 minutes.

5. Remove the cover and add the apricots and sherry. Turn up the heat
   and cook for 5 minutes allowing the liquid to reduce by half.
   Serve at once.

TO DRINK

Venison is most certainly
best with red wine.
Chilean, New Zealand,
Californian and
Argentinean
Cabernets are
all excellent.

RECIPE INFORMATION

RECIPE SERVES 4

Preparation - **20 minutes**
Cooking - **15 minutes**

AVERAGE VALUES PER PORTION
Calories - 435 kcals
Protein - 44g
Carbohydrate - 15g
Fat - 21g

COOK'S TIP

It is important to
cook the venison slowly.
If the heat is too high
the meat becomes
tough and stringy.

PAN FRIED VENISON WITH APRICOTS

THAI STYLE SATAY

Not the usual Malaysian Satay which uses peanuts, this Thai recipe is spicy and hot.
Those less acquainted with Thai recipes may wish to tone down the chilli.

Coconut milk	*100ml*
Garlic cloves	*3, crushed*
Coriander	*1 tablespoon*
Cumin seeds	*1 tablespoon*
Turmeric	*1 teaspoon*
Chilli sauce	*2 teaspoons*
Lime juice	*3 tablespoons*
Thai fish sauce	*3 tablespoons*
Soy sauce	*4 tablespoons*
Boneless chicken breasts	*4, skinned and cubed*

METHOD

1. Combine all the ingredients, except the chicken to make the sauce. Whisk until smooth.

2. Coat the chicken cubes in half the sauce and leave to marinate for 25 minutes. Place the remaining sauce in a shallow dish to serve as a dipping sauce with the kebabs. Meanwhile soak some wooden kebab sticks in cold water for at least 15 minutes.

3. Thread the chicken onto the kebab sticks and grill on a medium hot setting for about 15 minutes, turning occasionally so that the kebabs are evenly cooked.

4. When the kebabs are cooked and look golden, serve immediately with the dipping sauce.

TO DRINK

The powerful flavours here need careful matching: a dry fino sherry would have the necessary weight and zest.

RECIPE INFORMATION

RECIPE SERVES 4

Preparation - **25 minutes**
Cooking - **15 minutes**

AVERAGE VALUES PER PORTION
Calories - 195 kcals
Protein - 32g
Carbohydrate - 6g
Fat - 5g

COOK'S TIP

Soaking the wooden kebab sticks prevents them from drying out during cooking and burning.

THAI STYLE SATAY

PORK AND BEETROOT CASSEROLE

What may seem unusual is a wonderful fruity yet savoury casserole that puts others in the shade.

Allspice   *1 teaspoon*

Flour   *3 tablespoons*

Pork fillet   *500g, sliced*

Sunflower oil   *2 tablespoons*

Onion   *1 large, chopped*

Smoked bacon   *6 streaky rashers, chopped*

Vegetable stock   *600ml*

Oranges   *2 large, peeled and chopped*

Cooked beetroot   *250g, peeled and cubed*

Potatoes   *500g, peeled and cubed*

Fresh chives   *8 blades, snipped into*
Soured cream   *4 tablespoons*

Paprika   *1 teaspoon, to decorate*

METHOD

1. Mix the allspice with the flour and coat the pork.

2. Heat the oil in a casserole and brown the pork, remove and keep warm.

3. Fry the onion and bacon for 3 minutes. Add the pork back to the pan and pour in the stock. Bring to the boil and simmer.

4. Add the orange, beetroot and potatoes and cook for 30 minutes.

5. Take off the heat and stir. Add the soured cream and chives, sprinkle the paprika over the dish and serve.

TO DRINK

A Hungarian Pinot Gris is just the job for this unusual and flavoursome dish, or a full but fruity red wine like Morgon or Moulin à Vent.

RECIPE INFORMATION

RECIPE SERVES 4

Preparation - **5 minutes**
Cooking - **35 minutes**

AVERAGE VALUES PER PORTION
Calories - 630 kcals
Protein - 37g
Carbohydrate - 47g
Fat - 33g

COOK'S TIP

One rule:
The beetroot must be fresh not floating in vast quantities of vinegar!

PORK AND BEETROOT CASSEROLE

PHEASANT WITH BACON AND CHESTNUTS

Rich, warm and inviting - an autumnal treat.

Butter	*50g*
Vegetable oil	*1 tablespoon*
Young pheasants	*2, jointed to make 6 pieces each*
Onion	*1 large, sliced*
Bacon	*6 rashers, chopped*
Chestnuts	*125g, whole and peeled*
Plain flour	*40g*
Chicken stock	*450ml*
Red wine	*150ml*
Redcurrant jelly	*2 tablespoons*
Plain kettle crisps	*to accompany*

METHOD

1. Preheat the oven to 180°C. Heat the butter and oil in a casserole and brown the pheasant joints. Remove from the pan and keep warm.

2. Fry the onion, bacon and chestnuts in the juices, until golden brown.

3. Add the flour, stir well and heat for 2-3 minutes. Gradually add the chicken stock and red wine, slowly bring to the boil stirring all the time, until thickened.

4. Add the pheasant and redcurrant jelly, cover and cook for 30 minutes, until the pheasant is tender. Serve with warmed kettle crisps.

TO DRINK

Pheasant has a strong flavour and is best suited to red wine. Try Crozes-Hermitage or Rhône reds. Côte de Brouilly and Oregon Pinot Noir also go well.

RECIPE INFORMATION

RECIPE SERVES 4

Preparation - **10 minutes**
Cooking - **30 minutes**

AVERAGE VALUES PER PORTION
Calories - 850 kcals
Protein - 74g
Carbohydrate - 27g
Fat - 48g

COOK'S TIP

The season for fresh pheasant is from 1st October through to 1st February. Alternatively use frozen pheasants that have been thoroughly defrosted.

PHEASANT WITH BACON AND CHESTNUTS

ASPARAGUS SAFFRON RISOTTO WITH CHICKEN

*The wonderful combination of succulent chicken with fresh asparagus
and strands of aromatic saffron make this a pretty, summery dish.*

Butter	*15g*
Olive oil	*1 tablespoon*
Spanish onion	*1, finely chopped*
Arborio risotto rice	*300g*
Chicken stock	*850ml*
Saffron	*approx. 10 strands (1 teaspoon)*
White wine	*150ml*
Cooked chicken breasts	*2, roughly torn into strips*
Fresh asparagus	*130g, trimmed and sliced*
Parmesan cheese	*30g, freshly shaved*

METHOD

1. Heat the butter and oil in a heavy saucepan on a medium heat.
Add the onion and fry for 5 minutes until starting to brown.

2. Add the rice, half the stock and saffron and heat until almost boiling,
stirring so that the rice absorbs all the liquid and swells up.
This will take just a few minutes.

3. Gradually add the remaining stock, stir, cover and cook over a medium heat until
at least half the liquid has been absorbed. Add the wine and simmer for 3 minutes.

4. Add the chicken and stir. Cook for 5 minutes and add the asparagus.
Cook for another 5 minutes then add the cheese and serve.

TO DRINK

Unoaked white wines such as Chardonnay and Sauvignon Blanc go well with this dish.

RECIPE INFORMATION

RECIPE SERVES 4

Preparation - **10 minutes**
Cooking - **20 minutes**

AVERAGE VALUES PER PORTION
Calories - 570 kcals
Protein - 27g
Carbohydrate - 62g
Fat - 20g

COOK'S TIPS

Do not rinse Arborio rice in advance.

Should you need extra liquid, add extra chicken stock a little at a time.

Shave the Parmesan cheese using a vegetable peeler.

ASPARAGUS SAFFRON RISOTTO WITH CHICKEN

Oriental Duck Salad

This moist, aromatic dish brings out the full flavour of succulent duck which goes well with the stir fry ingredients served with a light salad to cleanse the palate.

Duck breasts   *2*

Hoisin sauce   *5 tablespoons*

Chilli sauce   *1 teaspoon*

Lambs leaf lettuce   *60g, washed*

French dressing   *1 teaspoon*

Sesame oil   *2 teaspoons*

Mangetout   *150g, trimmed*

Broccoli florets   *300g, trimmed*

Spring onions   *5, trimmed to 4cm (1½ inch) strips*

Soy sauce   *1 tablespoon*

METHOD

1. Place the duck in a roasting tin and add the hoisin and chilli sauces. Leave for at least 15 minutes. Preheat the oven to 220°C.

2. Cover the duck with foil and roast in the marinade for 15 minutes. Turn the oven off, remove the foil and leave the duck to continue cooking in the oven.

3. Toss the lettuce in the dressing and spoon onto serving plates.

4. Heat the oil in a wok and add the vegetables.

5. Stir fry the vegetables for 3-4 minutes and add the soy sauce.

6. Slice the duck breasts into about 6-8 pieces per breast. Spoon the stir fry next to the salad, add the duck slices and serve at once.

TO DRINK

The sweet rich taste of hoisin sauce with duck is best suited to full bodied spicy whites like Gewurztraminer, Viognier and Pinot Gris.

RECIPE INFORMATION

RECIPE SERVES 4

Preparation - **15 minutes**
Cooking - **19 minutes**

AVERAGE VALUES PER PORTION
Calories - 160 kcals
Protein - 5g
Carbohydrate - 14g
Fat - 4g

COOK'S TIP

Duck is an extremely fatty bird. To lessen the fat and produce a crispy skin, rinse the breasts and pat dry, then prick the skin all over. This allows the fat to drain out as it cooks.

ORIENTAL DUCK SALAD

MINTY LAMB

A fresh minty flavour combined with yogurt and a touch of garlic create a succulent dish.

Natural yogurt	*250g*
Garlic cloves	*3, crushed*
Mint sauce concentrate	*2 tablespoons*
Lamb chump chops	*8*
Fresh mint leaves	*to decorate*

METHOD

1. Combine the yogurt, garlic and mint sauce concentrate in a bowl and leave for 15 minutes to allow the flavours to develop.

2. Halve the mixture, placing one half in a serving bowl and the other half over the chops.

3. Grill the lamb chops on a medium-hot grill until thoroughly cooked, about 5 minutes each side.
Whilst the chops are cooking heat an ovenproof serving dish.

4. Drain the chops of any fat and place into the warmed serving dish. Decorate with the fresh mint leaves and serve with the minty-yogurt sauce.

TO DRINK

Lamb begs for a rich red Bordeaux wine, but the light, minty flavour of this dish allows you to experiment. Stick with Cabernet Sauvignon, but try a South African version.

RECIPE INFORMATION

RECIPE SERVES 4

Preparation - **15 minutes**
Cooking - **10 minutes**

AVERAGE VALUES PER PORTION
Calories - 725 kcals
Protein - 30g
Carbohydrate - 6g
Fat - 64g

COOK'S TIP

Lamb is a naturally fatty meat and it is therefore, important to drain off any excess fat. If necessary, pat the chops with kitchen paper.

MINTY LAMB

THAI GREEN CURRY

This Thai speciality uses green chillies, hence its name,
along with other flavoursome ingredients providing a dish quite different to an Indian curry.

Green curry paste	*2 tablespoons*
Garlic cloves	*2, quartered*
Ginger purée	*2 teaspoons*
Fresh green chillies	*2 small, deseeded and sliced*
Onion	*1 medium, quartered*
Fresh lemon grass	*1 blade, chopped*
Rump steak	*375g, sliced very thinly*
Sunflower oil	*1 tablespoon*
Coconut milk	*300ml*
Fresh coriander	*5 tablespoons, finely chopped*
Thai Jasmine rice	*to serve*

METHOD

1. Place the curry paste, garlic, ginger, chilli, onion and lemon grass in a blender or food processor and blend for 10 seconds until chunky. Stir with a spoon.

2. Place the beef in a bowl with the oil and add the blended paste. Mix well and leave to marinate for at least 30 minutes (the longer the better).

3. Heat a wok on a low heat and add the beef and the paste. Turn up the heat and add the coconut milk.

4. Cook the mixture for about 10 minutes stirring constantly. Add the coriander and cook for 30 seconds, serve with Thai Jasmine rice.

TO DRINK	RECIPE INFORMATION	COOK'S TIP
Ice cold lager matches the clean green flavours well. For adventure try a dry Sercial Madeira for its strong flavours.	RECIPE SERVES 4 Preparation - **30 minutes** Cooking - **11 minutes** AVERAGE VALUES PER PORTION Calories - 260 kcals Protein - 19g Carbohydrate - 8g Fat - 17g	If you like hot Thai food choose small green chillies and add some of the seeds. For those who like a slightly 'tamer' dish choose larger chillies and remove all seeds and pith.

THAI GREEN CURRY

Spiced Chicken, Banana and Coconut Salad

A delicious alternative to Coronation chicken - fruity, light and very easy to prepare.

Low fat mayonnaise *6 tablespoons*
Low fat natural yogurt *250ml*
Medium strength curry powder *1½ tablespoons*
Mango chutney *6 tablespoons*
Cooked chicken *600g, chopped into bite sized pieces*
Desiccated coconut *4 tablespoons*
Sultanas *40g*
Slivered almonds *30g*
Fresh mint *1 tablespoon, plus 2 sprigs to decorate*
Bananas *3, sliced and soaked in*
Lemon juice *2 tablespoons*
Crisp lettuce *to serve*

METHOD

1. Mix the mayonnaise, yogurt, curry powder and mango chutney in a bowl.

2. Spoon the sauce over the chicken and gently fold in.
Add the desiccated coconut and sultanas to the chicken.

3. Toast the almonds under a hot grill until starting to brown, about 2 minutes.

4. Meanwhile stir the fresh mint into the chicken. Add the bananas. Stir thoroughly.

5. Scatter the hot almonds over the dish and serve garnished with the fresh mint sprigs on a bed of crisp lettuce such as cos or little gem.

TO DRINK
Chilled tropical fruit juices go well with this dish, as would a sweeter white wine.

RECIPE INFORMATION
RECIPE SERVES 4
Preparation - **10 minutes**
Cooking - **2 minutes**
AVERAGE VALUES PER PORTION
Calories - 605 kcals
Protein - 44g
Carbohydrate - 51g
Fat - 25g

COOK'S TIP
This dish can be made in advance but don't add the bananas until you are ready to serve.

SPICED CHICKEN, BANANA AND COCONUT SALAD

LAMB KEBABS WITH TOMATO RICE

Marinated tender lamb with herbs on a bed of bright tomato rice.

Lamb fillet   *450g, trimmed and cubed*

Garlic and red wine marinade   *6 tablespoons*

Oil   *2 tablespoons*

Shallots   *3, diced*

Garlic cloves   *2, crushed*

Long grain rice   *220g, rinsed*

Bay leaf   *1, torn*

Dried mixed herbs   *1 tablespoon*

Vegetable stock   *375ml*

Chopped tomatoes with herbs   *1 large tin (400g)*

Frozen peas   *75g, defrosted*

Fresh thyme   *to decorate*

METHOD

1. Coat the lamb in the marinade and leave in a cool place for at least 15 minutes.

2. Meanwhile, heat the oil in a casserole and gently fry the shallots. After 2 minutes add the garlic, rice and herbs. Stir, add the stock and tomatoes, cover and simmer for 10 minutes.

3. Thread the lamb onto flat skewers. Preheat the grill to hot. Check the rice, if it requires extra fluid, add 1 tablespoon at a time to ensure the rice remains fluffy.

4. Grill the lamb for 3-4 minutes each side. Take the lid off the rice, add the peas, stir and cook for 1 minute, then decorate with thyme.

TO DRINK

An Italian Dolcetto is a good red wine that can stand up to the acidity of tomatoes, alternatively enjoy a bottle of Corbières or Côtes du Roussillon.

RECIPE INFORMATION

RECIPE SERVES 4

Preparation - **20 minutes**
Cooking - **10 minutes**

AVERAGE VALUES PER PORTION
Calories - 625 kcals
Protein - 38g
Carbohydrate - 59g
Fat - 28g

COOK'S TIP

You can buy premium marinade sauces from fine food stores and sometimes in butchers' shops.

Flat kebab skewers prevent the meat from spinning round whilst cooking.

LAMB KEBABS WITH TOMATO RICE

QUICK CHICKEN WITH WHITE WINE & MUSHROOMS

Even the most inexperienced cook will find this recipe so simple yet impressive.

Boneless chicken thighs	*8*
Chicken stock	*100ml*
Chestnut mushrooms	*110g, quartered*
Condensed soup mushroom with garlic	*1 tin (295g)*
White wine	*100ml*
Black pepper	*to season*
Parsley sprigs	*to garnish*

METHOD

1. Place the chicken in a heavy based casserole with
4 tablespoons of stock,
cover and cook for 8 minutes.

2. Add the mushrooms and remaining stock.
Cook for a further 4 minutes until almost boiling.

3. Turn down the heat and add the soup.
Stir, cover and cook for 5 minutes.

4. Add the wine, stir and season with pepper.
Cook uncovered for 3 minutes and serve
decorated with fresh parsley.

TO DRINK

A chilled Frascati,
Bordeaux Blanc or unoaked
Chardonnay will suit this
combination of
chicken and
mushrooms.

RECIPE INFORMATION

RECIPE SERVES 4

Preparation - **5 minutes**
Cooking - **20 minutes**

AVERAGE VALUES PER PORTION
Calories - 245 kcals
Protein - 29g
Carbohydrate - 5g
Fat - 10g

COOK'S TIP

There are a variety of
condensed soups in the
shops that can be used to
make a quick casserole.
We used a luxury variety
that contained mushrooms,
garlic and wine.

QUICK CHICKEN WITH WHITE WINE & MUSHROOMS

Stir Fried Pork in a Barbecue Sauce

Fresh vegetables and smoky barbecue sauce with the slices of pork make a quick stir fry supper.

Barbecue sauce	*6 tablespoons*
Pork loin steaks	*4, trimmed and sliced*
Spinach leaves	*1 bag (approx. 250g)*
Sunflower oil	*2 tablespoons*
Red onions	*2, cut into thick wedges*
Red pepper	*1, coarsely chopped*
Water	*50ml*

METHOD

1. Pour the barbecue sauce into a shallow dish.
Add the pork loin to the sauce and leave to marinate
for as long as possible (at least 30 minutes).

2. Remove the stalks from the spinach, rinse and then
leave in a colander.

3. Heat the oil in a wok or large frying pan and add the pork with the sauce.
Stir fry for 3 minutes and turn up the heat.
Separate the onion segments and add to the pork,
with the red pepper and water.

4. Stir fry for 3 minutes. Add the spinach leaves, let them wilt
then stir once or twice and serve.

TO DRINK

A Pinot Noir or
light Italian red wine
such as Valpolicella are
excellent with
this dish.

RECIPE INFORMATION

RECIPE SERVES 4

Preparation - **30 minutes**
Cooking - **7 minutes**

AVERAGE VALUES PER PORTION
Calories - 565 kcals
Protein - 25g
Carbohydrate - 13g
Fat - 46g

COOK'S TIP

Choose the best quality
barbecue sauce.
There are several
American brands that
stand out and have a good
hickory smoke flavour.

STIR FRIED PORK IN A BARBECUE SAUCE

BACON AND STILTON FRITTATA

*Unlike an omelet a frittata is firmer because it is cooked over a low heat and left round rather than folded.
Stilton and bacon are a great couple, with the sweetcorn taking the edge off the harshness of the Stilton.*

Oil	*2 tablespoons*
Red onion	*1, sliced*
Bacon	*6 rashers, trimmed and sliced*
Cooked new potatoes	*350g, sliced*
Creamed sweetcorn	*300g, from 1 large tin*
Fresh herbs	*2 tablespoons, plus sprigs to decorate*
Eggs	*4 large*
Quark	*5 tablespoons*
Stilton cheese	*60g, crumbled*

METHOD

1. Heat the oil in a large frying pan and fry the onion and bacon
until crisp and brown.

2. Add the potatoes to the pan and cook for 5 minutes.
Turn down the heat, add the sweetcorn and fresh herbs and stir.

3. Beat the eggs in a bowl, add the quark, whisk until well mixed and add the Stilton.

4. Pour into the pan and swill around until the vegetables and bacon are covered.

5. Cover and leave to cook on a low heat for 12 minutes. Preheat the grill on high.

6. Take the pan off the stove, uncover and place under the grill.
Warm through until the top has set and started to brown.
Scatter with remaining herbs and serve hot or cold.

TO DRINK	RECIPE INFORMATION	COOK'S TIP
Try a Beaujolais Villages or Australian Shiraz red wine which will stand up well to the strong flavours in this meal.	RECIPE SERVES 4 Preparation - **15 minutes** Cooking - **20 minutes** AVERAGE VALUES PER PORTION Calories - 475 kcals Protein - 21g Carbohydrate - 30g Fat - 32g	Quark is a very low fat soft cheese with a rich texture. If you are unable to find Quark, use mascarpone or cream cheese, but these may have a higher fat content, unless you buy low fat variants.

BACON AND STILTON FRITTATA

INDEX